W9-DJF-823

Merry Christmas!
Beverly Barras Vidrine

A Christmas Dictionary

A Christmas Dictionary

Beverly Barras Vidrine
Illustrated by Patrick Soper

PELICAN PUBLISHING COMPANY
Gretna 1998

First printing, September 1997
Second printing, September 1998

For my children, Denise, Bill, and Ken, who fill my life with happiness

*The word "Pelican" and the depiction of a pelican are trademarks
of Pelican Publishing Company, Inc., and are registered
in the U.S. Patent and Trademark Office.*

Library of Congress Cataloging-in-Publication Data

Vidrine, Beverly Barras.
   A Christmas dictionary / Beverly Barras Vidrine ; illustrated by
Patrick Soper.
      p.   cm.
   Summary: A dictionary in which every letter of the alphabet
represents some aspect of Christmas and its celebration.
   ISBN 1-56554-252-5 (alk. paper)
   1. Christmas—Dictionaries, Juvenile. [1. Christmas.
2. Alphabet.] I. Soper, Patrick, ill. II. Title.
GT4985.5.V54 1997
394.2663'03—dc21
[E]
                                97-7040
                                  CIP
                                  AC

Printed in Hong Kong

Published by Pelican Publishing Company, Inc.
1000 Burmaster Street, Gretna, Louisiana 70053

A Christmas Dictionary

The First Christmas

One night long ago shepherds were watching their sheep in a field. A bright star lit up the sky. An angel appeared before them. The angel said, "A baby named Jesus has been born. Jesus is a gift from God." The shepherds followed the star to a town called Bethlehem. The star led them to a stable. There they found the baby Jesus in a manger. He was wrapped in swaddling clothes. Mary and Joseph were next to him. Since then Christians have celebrated Christmas to remember the birthday of Jesus.

Advent

The four Sundays before Christmas are known as the Advent season. It is the time when Christians prepare for the birthday of Jesus.

Angel

A messenger of God is called an angel. An angel is often pictured with wings and a white robe.

Bells

Bells chime to call people to church. And ringing bells are part of Christmas. They are seen on Christmas cards and on wreaths. There are bell-shaped ornaments. Even Santa has sleigh bells.

Bible

God's words are written in a book called the Bible. The Bible has two parts—the Old Testament and the New Testament. The Old Testament tells what happened before the coming of Jesus. The New Testament tells about the life of Jesus.

Candle

It is said that the lighted Christmas candle stands for the Star of Bethlehem.

Carol

A song about Christmas is called a carol. A well-known Christmas carol is "Silent Night."

Christmas

The word "Christmas" means *Christ's Mass.* This is the special church service that honors the birth of Jesus. The holiday has a serious side for Christians. It is to remember Jesus on his birthday. The Christmas season has a fun side too. Families shop for gifts. They trim Christmas trees and hang stockings. Many boys and girls write Christmas lists. And little children look forward to Santa's visit.

Candle

December 25

Christmas is December 25. Christians celebrate the birthday of Jesus on this day.

Dickens, Charles

Charles Dickens was an author. He lived in England over a hundred years ago. His most famous story is called *A Christmas Carol.* The story is about Scrooge. He was mean and didn't like Christmas. But by the end of the story he changes his mind. And Scrooge discovers the true meaning of Christmas, which is goodwill toward others.

Elves

Elves are pictured as tiny old-looking people. Christmas elves often wear red suits. It is said that they make toys in Santa's workshop at the North Pole.

Epiphany

The last day of the Christmas season is called Epiphany. This feast is celebrated on January 6.

Evergreen

A plant that is green all year is called evergreen. Some evergreen plants, like ivy, are used for Christmas decorations. Pine trees and fir trees are evergreens. They are popular Christmas trees.

Frosty the Snowman

The name of a well-liked Christmas song is "Frosty the Snowman." This jolly tune is about a snowman named Frosty coming to life.

Fruitcake

A favorite food during the Christmas holidays is the fruitcake. This rich cake is made of nuts, fruits, and spices.

ift-giving

People trade gifts at Christmas. And Santa Claus brings presents to boys and girls. Gift-giving is a way to show our love for family and friends.

God's Gift

Jesus is God's gift to all people. We celebrate the birth of Jesus at Christmastime. This celebration helps us to know God's love.

Greetings

People welcome the holiday with greetings. They say, "Merry Christmas" to friends and family. Some send Christmas cards with happy messages.

Holiday

A day of freedom from work and school is called a holiday. Christmas is a favorite holiday.

olly

Holly

The holly bush is an evergreen plant. It has the colors of Christmas. Its leaves are green and its berries are red. Holly branches are often used for Christmas decorations.

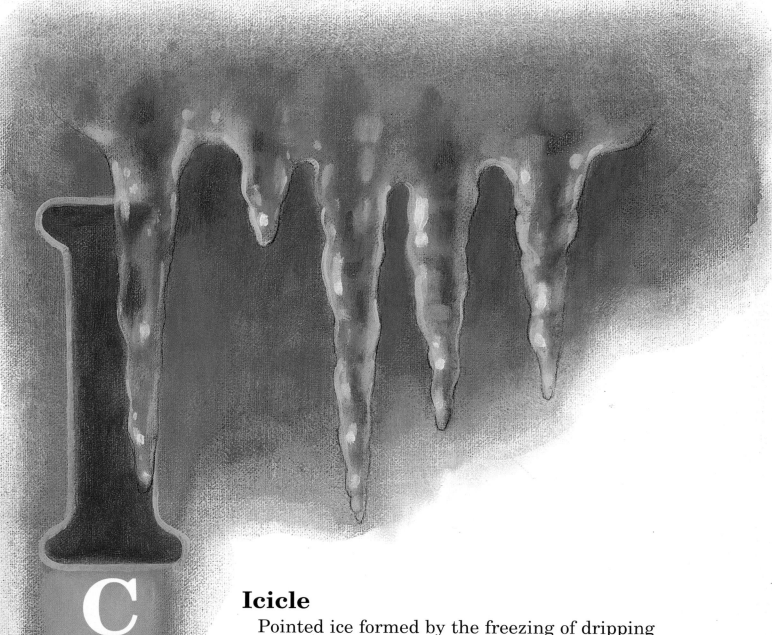

Icicle

Pointed ice formed by the freezing of dripping water is called an icicle. At Christmas thin strips of silver foil are made to look like icicles. Gleaming icicles are used as ornaments on Christmas trees.

Indiana

The state of Indiana has a town called Santa Claus. Its theme park is called Holiday World. The park has a Santa's workshop. It also has the world's largest statue of Santa Claus. It is almost as tall as a two-story house. Almost everything in Santa Claus, Indiana, has a Christmas name.

Jesus

The Son of God is Jesus. He is also called Christ. Jesus Christ was born almost two thousand years ago.

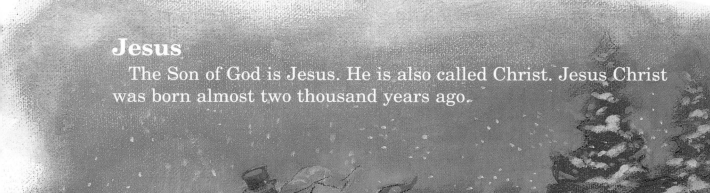

The name of a popular Christmas song is "Jingle Bells." The song tells about bells tied to a sleigh and to the harness of a horse. They jingle as the horse pulls the sleigh, full of happy people, across the snow.

Joseph

Joseph was the husband of Mary. He worked as a carpenter.

Kindness

Kindness to others is shown at Christmas. People give food and clothes to the needy. Groups visit hospitals and nursing homes. They sing carols and give presents. People make special efforts to see that others have a Merry Christmas.

Kriss Kringle

Kriss Kringle

Another name for Santa Claus is Kriss Kringle. He got that nickname long ago when German people came to America. On Christmas Eve they received presents from the Christ child. But they called the Christ child *Christkindl*. Some people changed the name to Kriss Kringle. Santa has many other names. A few are Father Christmas, Papa Noel, Saint Nicholas, Saint Nick, and Sinterklaas.

Lights

Lights

Thomas Edison invented electric lights in the year 1879. A few years later his friend Edward Johnson had the first Christmas tree lit by electricity. Bulbs blinked and an electrically powered stand turned the tree around. Soon after, businesses sold strings of ready-made lights.

Manger

A feedbox in a stable is called a manger. Jesus was laid in a manger at his birth.

Mistletoe

Mistletoe

An evergreen with clusters of white berries is called mistletoe. It grows on bushes and trees without ever touching the ground. The mistletoe is a sign of happiness and love. Sometimes it is hung above doorways. A popular Christmas custom is for people to kiss under the mistletoe.

Nativity

The birth of Jesus at Bethlehem is called the Nativity. The Nativity scene shows Baby Jesus lying in a manger. Mary and Joseph are next to him. Often the shepherds, animals, angels, and the bright Star of Bethlehem are nearby.

Noel

The French word for "Christmas" is *Noël*. The song "The First Noel" tells the story of the first Christmas.

North Pole

It is said that Santa Claus lives at the North Pole. This most northern part of the earth is covered with snow and ice.

Ornaments

Decorations on Christmas trees are called ornaments. They can be handmade or store bought. Some favorites are glass balls and icicles. Ornaments make Christmas trees beautiful.

Outdoor Christmas Trees

The first outdoor Christmas tree in America had electric lights. It was set up in Pasadena, California, in 1909. In 1923, the tradition of lighting a tree on the White House lawn began. Every Christmas season, the lights are turned on by the president of the United States.

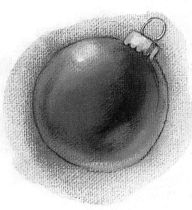

Peace on Earth

Angels sang of peace on earth the day Jesus was born. Christmas is a time of harmony among people. Even those who are angry with each other sometimes make up. There is peace on earth for a few days.

Piñata

The piñata is a Christmas tradition of Mexico. It is a decorated paper container filled with candies and toys. The piñata comes in all sizes and shapes. Some are clowns or animals. Usually it hangs from a ceiling. Then blindfolded children try to break it with a stick. Once it cracks open, the good things fall down. The children scramble for them.

Poinsettia

The poinsettia is a popular Christmas plant. Its green leaves turn red. The poinsettia comes from Mexico. The Mexican name means "Flower of the Holy Night." It was named "poinsettia" in America after the man who brought it here.

ueen of Heaven

The mother of Jesus is Mary. She has been honored as queen of heaven and earth.

Reindeer

A kind of deer that lives around the North Pole is called a reindeer. It is said that a team of reindeer pulls Santa's sleigh. In the poem *The Night Before Christmas,* the reindeer fly through the sky. Saint Nicholas calls them by name: "Now, Dasher! Now, Dancer! Now, Prancer and Vixen! On, Comet! On, Cupid! On, Donner and Blitzen!"

Saint Nicholas

Nicholas was a bishop in Europe a long time ago. He was kind to children and gave them gifts. He became known as a saint of children.

anta
Claus

Santa Claus

Santa Claus is Saint Nicholas. The Dutch word *Sinterklaas* means "Saint Nicholas." Long ago when American children said "Sinterklaas," it sounded like "Santa Claus." Today Santa Claus is well known as a jolly man who laughs, "Ho, ho, ho!" He has a long white beard. He wears a long cap and a red suit with black boots. And he carries a pack full of toys.

Sleigh

A wagon with runners is called a sleigh. It is used to carry people over ice or snow. The poem *The Night Before Christmas* tells about Saint Nicholas riding in a sleigh. Reindeer pull his sleigh full of toys.

Toys

Christmas is a time for toys. Some best-loved Christmas toys are stuffed animals. Others are dolls, bikes, and trains. On Christmas morning children rush to see their toys and presents under the tree. They find their stockings filled with playthings, fruit, and candy.

Trees

Many families decorate evergreen trees with strings of lights and ornaments. Some go to the woods or to tree farms and cut their own Christmas trees before trimming them.

United States

Christmas in the United States is special. Many Christmas customs in the United States came from the English, Dutch, and German settlers. These customs mixed together here.

Universal

Something that happens all over the world is called universal. Christmas is universal. People celebrate Christmas at different times. But they share many of the same customs.

Up on the Housetop

A popular old Christmas carol is called "Up on the Housetop." This song is about Santa and his reindeer on the roof of a house. Then Santa goes down the chimney with toys and fills the stockings.

Virgin Mary

The mother of Jesus is called the Virgin Mary or the Blessed Virgin Mary. Her feast day is May 31.

Visit from St. Nicholas

A long time ago, a Christmas poem called *A Visit from St. Nicholas* was written. Later the name was changed to *The Night Before Christmas*. Dr. Clement Moore wrote this poem as a bedtime story for his children. It is about a man who sees St. Nicholas coming down the chimney with a bag of presents. It is now famous. A funny imitation of this poem is *Cajun Night Before Christmas*.

Wassailers

People who go from house to house singing Christmas carols are called wassailers. They enjoy a punch called wassail after singing carols.

Wise Men

The Wise Men were travelers from the East. They followed a star that led them to Jesus. The Wise Men brought Jesus gifts of gold, frankincense, and myrrh. They are also known as the Three Kings.

Wreath

Something twisted into the shape of a circle is called a wreath. Christmas wreaths can be made of cloth, pine cones, straw, or branches from evergreen trees. Christmas wreaths are hung on doors as a sign of welcome.

mas

The word "Christmas" can be shortened to "Xmas." The *X* is the Greek sign for Christ.

Yule

Yule is another word for Christmas. Yule is the feast of the Nativity of Jesus Christ.

Yule Log

A huge log burned at Christmas is called a Yule log. Long ago in northern Europe people burned these logs for light and warmth.

Yuletide

Yuletide is another word for Christmastime.